Christopher Columbus
And The New World of His Discovery
Volume 6

FILSON YOUNG

[ZHINGOORA BOOKS]

This edition is published by
Zhingoora Books.

About Author

Alexander Bell Filson Young was a journalist, BBC programme advisor and author. His wrote the book on Titanic, a RMS Titanic ship. His famous works includeTitanic, The Relief of Mafekingand etc.

CHAPTER V

THE THIRD VOYAGE

Columbus was at sea again; firm ground to him, although so treacherous and unstable to most of us; and as he saw the Spanish coast sinking down on the horizon he could shake himself free from his troubles, and feel that once more he was in a situation of which he was master. He first touched at Porto Santo, where, if the story of his residence there be true, there must have been potent memories for him in the sight of the long white beach and the plantations, with the Governor's house beyond. He stayed there only a few hours and then crossed over to Madeira, anchoring in the Bay of Funchal, where he took in wood and water. As it was really unnecessary for him to make a port so soon after leaving, there was probably some other reason for his visit to these islands; perhaps a family reason; perhaps nothing more historically important than the desire to look once more on scenes of bygone happiness, for even on the page of history every event is not necessarily big with significance. From Madeira he took a southerly course to the Canary Islands, and on June 16th anchored at Gomera, where he found a French warship with two Spanish prizes, all of which put to sea as the Admiral's fleet approached. On June 21st, when he sailed from Gomera, he divided his fleet of six vessels into two squadrons. Three ships were despatched direct to Espanola, for the supplies which they carried were urgently needed there. These three ships were commanded by trustworthy men: Pedro de Arana, a brother of Beatriz, Alonso Sanchez de Carvajal, and Juan Antonio Colombo—this last no other than a cousin of Christopher's from Genoa. The sons of Domenico's provident younger brother had not prospered, while the sons of improvident Domenico were now all in high places; and these three poor cousins, hearing of Christopher's greatness, and deciding that use should be made of him, scraped together enough money to send one of their number to Spain. The Admiral always had a sound family feeling, and finding that cousin Antonio had sea experience and knew how to handle a ship he gave him command of one of the caravels on this voyage—a command of which he proved capable and worthy. From these three captains, after giving them full sailing directions for reaching Espanola, Columbus parted company off the island of Ferro. He himself stood on a southerly course towards the Cape Verde Islands.

His plan on this voyage was to find the mainland to the southward, of which he had heard rumours in Espanola. Before leaving Spain he had received a letter from an eminent lapidary named Ferrer who had travelled much in the east, and who assured him that if he sought gold and precious stones he must go to hot lands, and that the hotter the lands were, and the blacker the inhabitants, the more likely he was to find riches there. This was just the kind of theory to suit Columbus, and as he sailed towards the Cape Verde Islands he was already in imagination gathering gold and pearls on the shores of the equatorial continent.

He stayed for about a week at the Cape Verde Islands, getting in provisions and cattle, and curiously observing the life of the Portuguese lepers who came in numbers to the island of Buenavista to be cured there by eating the flesh and bathing in the blood of turtles. It was not an inspiriting week which he spent in that dreary place and enervating climate, with nothing to see but the goats feeding among the scrub, the turtles crawling about the sand, and the lepers following the turtles. It began to tell on the health of the crew, so he weighed anchor on July 5th and stood on a southwesterly course.

This third voyage, which was destined to be the most important of all, and the material for which had cost him so much time and labour, was undertaken in a very solemn and determined spirit. His health, which he had hoped to recover in Spain, had been if anything damaged by his worryings with officialdom there; and although he was only forty-seven years of age he was in some respects already an old man. He had entered, although happily he did not know it, on the last decade of his life; and was already beginning to suffer from the two diseases, gout and ophthalmia, which were soon to undermine his strength and endurance. Religion of a mystical fifteenth-century sort was deepening in him; he had undertaken this voyage in the name of the Holy Trinity; and to that theological entity he had resolved to dedicate the first new land that he should sight.

For ten days light baffling winds impeded his progress; but at the end of that time the winds fell away altogether, and the voyagers found themselves in that flat equatorial calm known to mariners as the Doldrums. The vertical rays of the sun shone blisteringly down upon them, making the seams of the ships gape and causing the unhappy crews mental as well as bodily distress, for they began to fear that they had reached that zone of fire which had always been said to exist in the southern ocean.

Day after day the three ships lay motionless on the glassy water, with wood-work so hot as to burn the hands that touched it, with the meat putrefying in the casks below, and the water running from the loosened casks, and no one with courage and endurance enough to venture into the stifling hold even to save the provisions. And through all this the Admiral, racked with gout, had to keep a cheerful face and assure his prostrate crew that they would soon be out of it.

There were showers of rain sometimes, but the moisture in that baking atmosphere only added to its stifling and enervating effects. All the while, however, the great slow current of the Atlantic was moving westward, and there came a day when a heavenly breeze, stirred in the torrid air and the musical talk of ripples began to rise again from the weedy stems of the ships. They sailed due west, always into a cooler and fresher atmosphere; but still no land was sighted, although pelicans and smaller birds were continually seen passing from south-west to north-east. As provisions were beginning to run low, Columbus decided on the 31st July to alter his course to north-by-east, in the hope of reaching the island of Dominica. But at mid-day his servant Alonso Perez, happening to go to the masthead, cried out that there was land in sight; and sure enough to the westward there rose three peaks of land united at the base. Here was the kind of coincidence which staggers even the unbeliever. Columbus had promised to dedicate the first land he saw to the Trinity; and here was the land, miraculously provided when he needed it most, three peaks in one peak, in due conformity with the requirements of the blessed Saint Athanasius. The Admiral was deeply affected; the God of his belief was indeed a good friend to him; and he wrote down his pious conviction that the event was a miracle, and summoned all hands to sing the Salve Regina, with other hymns in praise of God and the Virgin Mary. The island was duly christened La Trinidad. By the hour of Compline (9 o'clock in the evening) they had come up with the south coast of the island, but it was the next day before the Admiral found a harbour where he could take in water. No natives were to be seen, although there were footprints on the shore and other signs of human habitation.

He continued all day to sail slowly along the shore of the island, the green luxuriance of which astonished him; and sometimes he stood out from the coast to the southward as he made a long board to round this or that point. It must have been while reaching out in this way to the southward that he saw a low shore on his port hand some sixty miles to the south of Trinidad, and that his sight, although he did not know it, rested for the first time on the mainland of South America. The land seen was the low coast to the west of the Orinoco, and thinking that it was an island he gave it the name of Isla Sancta.

On the 2nd of August they were off the south-west of Trinidad, and saw the first inhabitants in the shape of a canoe full of armed natives, who approached the ships with threatening gestures. Columbus had brought out some musicians with him, possibly for the purpose of impressing the natives, and perhaps with the idea of making things a little more cheerful in Espanola; and the musicians were now duly called upon to give a performance, a tambourine-player standing on the forecastle and beating the rhythm for the ships' boys to dance to. The effect was other than was anticipated, for the natives immediately discharged a thick flight of arrows at the musicians, and the music and dancing abruptly ceased. Eventually the Indians were prevailed upon to come on board the two smaller ships and to receive gifts, after which they departed and were seen no more. Columbus landed and made some observations of the vegetation and climate of Trinidad, noticing that the fruits and trees were similar to those of Espanola, and that oysters abounded, as well as "very large, infinite fish, and parrots as large as hens."

He saw another peak of the mainland to the northwest, which was the peninsula of Paria, and to which Columbus, taking it to be another island, gave the name of Isla de Gracia. Between him and this land lay a narrow channel through which a mighty current was flowing—that press of waters which, sweeping across the Atlantic from Africa, enters the Caribbean Sea, sprays round the Gulf of Mexico, and turns north again in the current known as the Gulf Stream. While his ships were anchored at the entrance to this channel and Columbus was wondering how he should cross it, a mighty flood of water suddenly came down with a roar, sending a great surging wave in front of it. The vessels were lifted up as though by magic; two of them dragged their anchors from the bottom, and the other one broke her cable. This flood was probably caused by a sudden flush of fresh water from one of the many mouths of the Orinoco; but to Columbus, who had no thought of rivers in his mind, it was very alarming. Apparently, however, there was nothing for it but to get through the channel, and having sent boats on in front to take soundings and see that there was clear water he eventually piloted his little squadron through, with his heart in his mouth and his eyes fixed on the swinging eddies and surging circles of the channel. Once beyond it he was in the smooth water of the Gulf of Paria. He followed the westerly coast of Trinidad to the north until he came to a second channel narrower than the first, through which the current boiled with still greater violence, and to which he gave the name of Dragon's Mouth. This is the channel between the northwesterly point of Trinidad and the eastern promontory of Paria. Columbus now began to be bewildered, for he discovered that the water over the ship's side was fresh water, and he could not make out where it came from. Thinking that the peninsula of Paria was an island, and not wishing to attempt the dangerous passage of the Dragon's Mouth, he decided to coast along the southern shore of the land opposite, hoping to be able to turn north round its western extremity.

Sweeter blew the breezes, fresher grew the water, milder and more balmy the air, greener and deeper the vegetation of this beautiful region. The Admiral was ill with the gout, and suffering such pain from his eyes that he was sometimes blinded by it;

but the excitement of the strange phenomena surrounding him kept him up, and his powers of observation, always acute, suffered no diminution. There were no inhabitants to be seen as they sailed along the coast, but monkeys climbed and chattered in the trees by the shore, and oysters were found clinging to the branches that dipped into the water. At last, in a bay where they anchored to take in water, a native canoe containing three, men was seen cautiously approaching; and the men, who were shy, were captured by the device of a sailor jumping on to the gunwale of the canoe and overturning it, the natives being easily caught in the water, and afterwards soothed and captivated by the unfailing attraction of hawks' bells. They were tall men with long hair, and they told Columbus that the name of their country was Paria; and when they were asked about other inhabitants they pointed to the west and signified that there was a great population in that direction.

On the 10th of August 1498 a party landed on this coast and formally took possession of it in the name of the Sovereigns of Spain. By an unlucky chance Columbus himself did not land. His eyes were troubling him so much that he was obliged to lie down in his cabin, and the formal act of possession was performed by a deputy. If he had only known! If he could but have guessed that this was indeed the mainland of a New World that did not exist even in his dreams, what agonies he would have suffered rather than permit any one else to pronounce the words of annexation! But he lay there in pain and suffering, his curious mystical mind occupied with a conception very remote indeed from the truth.

For in that fertile hotbed of imagination, the Admiral's brain, a new and staggering theory had gradually been taking shape. As his ships had been wafted into this delicious region, as the airs had become sweeter, the vegetation more luxuriant, and the water of the sea fresher,—he had solemnly arrived at the conclusion that he was approaching the region of the true terrestrial Paradise: the Garden of Eden that some of the Fathers had declared to be situated in the extreme east of the Old World, and in a region so high that the flood had not overwhelmed it. Columbus, thinking hard in his cabin, blood and brain a little fevered, comes to the conclusion that the world is not round but pear-shaped. He knows that all this fresh water in the sea must come from a great distance and from no ordinary river; and he decides that its volume and direction have been acquired in its fall from the apex of the pear, from the very top of the world, from the Garden of Eden itself. It was a most beautiful conception; a theory worthy to be fitted to all the sweet sights and sounds in the world about him; but it led him farther and farther away from the truth, and blinded him to knowledge and understanding of what he had actually accomplished.

He had thought the coast of Cuba the mainland, and he now began to consider it at least possible that the peninsula of Paria was mainland also—another part of the same continent. That was the truth—Paria was the mainland—and if he had not been so bemused by his dreams and theories he might have had some inkling of the real wonder and significance of his discovery. But no; in his profoundly unscientific mind there was little of that patience which holds men back from theorising and keeps them ready to receive the truth. He was patient enough in doing, but in thinking he was not patient at all. No sooner had he observed a fact than he must find a theory which would bring it into relation with the whole of his knowledge; and if the facts would not harmonise of themselves he invented a scheme of things by which they were forced into harmony. He was indeed a Darwinian before his time, an adept in the art of inventing causes to fit facts, and then proving that the facts sprang from the causes; but his origins were tangible, immovable things of rock and soil that could be seen and visited by other men, and their true relation to the terrestrial phenomena accurately established; so that his very proofs were monumental, and became themselves the advertisements of his profound misjudgment. But meanwhile he is the Admiral of the Ocean Seas, and can "make it so"; and accordingly, in a state of mental instability, he makes the Gulf of Paria to be a slope of earth immediately below the Garden of Eden, although fortunately he does not this time provide a sworn affidavit of trembling ships' boys to confirm his discovery.

Meanwhile also here were pearls; the native women wore ropes of them all over their bodies, and a fair store of them were bartered for pieces of broken crockery. Asked as usual about the pearls the natives, also as usual, pointed vaguely to the west and south-west, and explained that there were more pearls in that direction. But the Admiral would not tarry. Although he believed that he was within reach of Eden and pearls, he was more anxious to get back to Espanola and send the thrilling news to Spain than he was to push on a little farther and really assure himself of the truth. How like Christopher that was! Ideas to him were of more value than facts, as indeed they are to the world at large; but one is sometimes led to wonder whether he did not sometimes hesitate to turn his ideas into facts for very fear that they should turn out to be only ideas. Was he, in his relations with Spain and the world, a trader in the names rather than the substance of things? We have seen him going home to Spain and announcing the discovery of the Golden Chersonesus, although he had only discovered what he erroneously supposed to be an indication of it; proclaiming the discovery of the Ophir of Solomon without taking the trouble to test for himself so tremendous an assumption; and we now see him hurrying away to dazzle Spain with the story that he has discovered the Garden of Eden, without even trying to push on for a few days more to secure so much as a cutting from the Tree of Life.

These are grave considerations; for although happily the Tree of Life is now of no importance to any human being, the doings of Admiral Christopher were of great importance to himself and to his fellow-men at that time, and are still to-day, through the infinite channels in which human thought and action run and continue thoughout the world, of grave importance to us. Perhaps this is not quite the moment, now that the poor Admiral is lying in pain and weakness and not quite master of his own mind, to consider fully how he stands in this matter of honesty; we will leave it for the present until he is well again, or better still, until his tale of life and action is complete, and comes as a whole before the bar of human judgment.

On August 11th Columbus turned east again after having given up the attempt to find a passage to the north round Paria. There were practical considerations that brought him to this action. As the water was growing shoaler and shoaler he had sent a caravel of light draft some way further to the westward, and she reported that there lay ahead of her a great inner bay or gulf consisting of almost entirely fresh water. Provisions, moreover, were running short, and were, as usual, turning bad; the Admiral's health made vigorous action of any kind impossible for him; he was anxious about the condition of Espanola—anxious also, as we have seen, to send this great news home; and he therefore turned back and decided to risk the passage of the Dragon's Mouth. He anchored in the neighbouring harbour until the wind was in the right quarter, and with some trepidation put his ships into the boiling tideway. When they were in the middle of the passage the wind fell to a dead calm, and the ships, with their sails hanging loose, were borne on the dizzy surface of eddies, overfalls, and whirls of the tide. Fortunately there was deep water in the passage, and the strength of the current carried them safely through. Once outside they bore away to the northward, sighting the islands of Tobago and Grenada and, turning westward again, came to the islands of Cubagua and Margarita, where three pounds of pearls were bartered from the natives. A week after the passage of the Dragon's Mouth Columbus sighted the south coast of Espanola, which coast he made at a point a long way to the east of the new settlement that he had instructed Bartholomew to found; and as the winds were contrary, and he feared it might take him a long time to beat up against them, he sent a boat ashore with a letter which was to be delivered by a native messenger to the Adelantado. The letter was delivered; a few days later a caravel was sighted which contained Bartholomew himself; and once more, after a long separation, these two friends and brothers were united.

The see-saw motion of all affairs with which Columbus had to do was in full swing. We have seen him patching up matters in Espanola; hurrying to Spain just in time to rescue his damaged reputation and do something to restore it; and now when he had come back it was but a sorry tale that Bartholomew had to tell him. A fortress had been built at the Hayna gold-mines, but provisions had been so scarce that there had been something like a famine among the workmen there; no digging had been done, no planting, no making of the place fit for human occupation and industry. Bartholomew had been kept busy in collecting the native tribute, and in planning out the beginnings of the settlement at the mouth of the river Ozema, which was at first called the New Isabella, but was afterwards named San Domingo in honour of old Domenico at Savona. The cacique Behechio had been giving trouble; had indeed marched out with an army against Bartholomew, but had been more or less reconciled by the intervention of his sister Anacaona, widow of the late Caonabo, who had apparently transferred her affections to Governor Bartholomew. The battle was turned into a friendly pagan festival—one of the last ever held on that once happy island—in which native girls danced in a green grove, with the beautiful Anacaona, dressed only in garlands, carried on a litter in their midst.

But in the Vega Real, where a chapel had been built by the priests of the neighbouring settlement who were beginning to make converts, trouble had arisen in consequence of an outrage on the wife of the cacique Guarionex. The chapel was raided, the shrine destroyed, and the sacred vessels carried off. The Spaniards seized a number of Indians whom they suspected of having had a hand in the desecration, and burned them at the stake in the most approved manner of the Inquisition—a hideous punishment that fanned the remaining embers of the native spirit into flame, and produced a hostile combination of Guarionex and several other caciques, whose rebellion it took the Adelantado some trouble and display of arms to quench.

But the worst news of all was the treacherous revolt of Francisco Roldan, a Spaniard who had once been a servant of the Admiral's, and who had been raised by him to the office of judge in the island—an able creature, but, like too many recipients of Christopher's favour, a treacherous rascal at bottom. As soon as the Admiral's back was turned Roldan had begun to make mischief, stirring up the discontent that was never far below the surface of life in the colony, and getting together a large band of rebellious ruffians. He had a plan to murder Bartholomew Columbus and place himself at the head of the colony, but this fell through. Then, in Bartholomew's absence, he had a passage with James Columbus, who had now returned to the island and had resumed his. official duties at Isabella. Bartholomew, who was at another part of the coast collecting tribute, had sent a caravel laden with cotton to Isabella, and well-meaning James had her drawn up on the beach. Roldan took the opportunity to represent this innocent action as a sign of the intolerable autocracy of the Columbus family, who did not even wish a vessel to be in a condition to sail for

Spain with news of their misdeeds. Insolent Roldan formally asks James to send the caravel to Spain with supplies; poor James refuses and, perhaps being at bottom afraid of Roldan and his insolences, despatches him to the Vega Real with a force to bring to order some caciques who had been giving trouble. Possibly to his surprise, although not to ours, Roldan departs with alacrity at the head of seventy armed men. Honest, zealous James, no doubt; but also, we begin to fear, stupid James.

The Vega Real was the most attractive part of the colony, and the scene of infinite idleness and debauchery in the early days of the Spanish settlement. As Margarite and other mutineers had acted, so did Roldan and his soldiers now act, making sallies against several of the chain of forts that stretched across the island, and even upon Isabella itself; and returning to the Vega to the enjoyment of primitive wild pleasures. Roldan and Bartholomew Columbus stalked each other about the island with armed forces for several months, Roldan besieging Bartholomew in the fortress at the Vega, which he had occupied in Roldan's absence, and trying to starve him out there. The arrival in February 1498 of the two ships which had been sent out from Spain in advance, and which brought also the news of the Admiral's undamaged favour at Court, and of the royal confirmation of Bartholomew's title, produced for the moment a good moral effect; Roldan went and sulked in the mountains, refusing to have any parley or communication with the Adelantado, declining indeed to treat with any one until the Admiral himself should return. In the meantime his influence with the natives was strong enough to produce a native revolt, which Bartholomew had only just succeeded in suppressing when Christopher arrived on August 30th.

The Admiral was not a little distressed to find that the three ships from which he had parted company at Ferro had not yet arrived. His own voyage ought to have taken far longer than theirs; they had now been nine weeks at sea, and there was nothing to account for their long delay. When at last they did appear, however they brought with them only a new complication. They had lost their way among the islands and had been searching about for Espanola, finally making a landfall there on the coast of Xaragua, the south-western province of the island, where Roldan and his followers were established. Roldan had received them and, concealing the fact of his treachery, procured a large store of provisions from them, his followers being meanwhile busy among the crews of the ships inciting them to mutiny and telling them of the oppression of the Admiral's rule and the joys of a lawless life. The gaol-birds were nothing loth; after eight weeks at sea a spell ashore in this pleasant land, with all kinds of indulgences which did not come within the ordinary regimen of convicts and sailors, greatly appealing to them. The result was that more than half of the crews mutinied and joined Roldan, and the captains were obliged to put to sea with their small loyal remnant. Carvajal remained behind in order to try to persuade Roldan to give himself up; but Roldan had no such idea, and Carvajal had to make his way by land to San Domingo, where he made his report to the Admiral. Roldan has in fact delivered a kind of ultimatum. He will surrender to no one but the Admiral, and that only on condition that he gets a free pardon. If negotiations are opened, Roldan will treat with no one but Carvajal. The Admiral, whose grip of the situation is getting weaker and weaker, finds himself in a difficulty. His loyal army is only some seventy strong, while Roldan has, of disloyal settlers, gaol-birds, and sailors, much more than that. The Admiral, since he cannot reduce his enemy's force by capturing them, seeks to do it by bribing them; and the greatest bribe that he can think of to offer to these malcontents is that any who like may have a free passage home in the five caravels which are now waiting to return to Spain. To such a pass have things come in the paradise of Espanola! But the rabble finds life pleasant enough in Xaragua, where they are busy with indescribable pleasures; and for the moment there is no great response to this invitation to be gone. Columbus therefore despatches his ships, with such rabble of colonists, gaol-birds, and mariners as have already had their fill both of pain and pleasure, and writes his usual letter to the Sovereigns—half full of the glories of the new discoveries he has made, the other half setting forth the evil doings of Roldan, and begging that he may be summoned to Spain for trial there. Incidentally, also, he requests a further licence for two years for the capture and despatch of slaves to Spain. So the vessels sail back on October 18, 1498, and the Admiral turns wearily to the task of disentangling the web of difficulty that has woven itself about him.

Carvajal and Ballester—another loyal captain—were sent with a letter to Roldan urging him to come to terms, and Carvajal and Ballester added their own honest persuasions. But Roldan was firm; he wished to be quit of the Admiral and his rule, and to live independently in the island; and of his followers, although some here and there showed signs of submission, the greater number were so much in love with anarchy that they could not be counted upon. For two months negotiations of a sort were continued, Roldan even presenting himself under a guarantee of safety at San Domingo, where he had a fruitless conference with the Admiral; where also he had an opportunity of observing what a sorry state affairs in the capital were in, and what a mess Columbus was making of it all. Roldan, being a simple man, though a rascal, had only to remain firm in order to get his way against a mind like the Admiral's, and get his way he ultimately did. The Admiral made terms of a kind most humiliating to him, and utterly subversive of his influence and authority. The mutineers were not only to receive a pardon but a certificate (good Heavens!) of good conduct. Caravels were to be sent to convey them to Spain; and they were to be permitted to carry with them all the slaves that they had collected and all the native young women whom they had ravished from their homes.

Columbus signs this document on the 21st of November, and promises that the ships shall be ready in fifty days; and then, at his wits' end, and hearing of irregularities in the interior of the island, sets off with Bartholomew to inspect the posts and restore them to order. In his absence the see-saw, in due obedience to the laws that govern all see-saws, gives a lurch to the other side, and things go all wrong again in San Domingo. The preparations for the despatch of the caravels are neglected as soon as his back is turned; not fifty days, but nearly one hundred days elapse before they are ready to sail from San Domingo to Xaragua. Even then they are delayed by storms and head-winds; and when they do arrive Roldan and his company will not embark in them. The agreement has been broken; a new one must be made. Columbus, returning to San Domingo after long and harassing struggles on the other end of the see-saw, gets news of this deadlock, and at the same time has news from Fonseca in Spain of a far from agreeable character. His complaints against the people under him have been received by the Sovereigns and will be duly considered, but their Majesties have not time at the moment to go into them. That is the gist of it, and very cold cheer it is for the Admiral, balancing himself on this turbulent see-saw with anxious eyes turned to Spain for encouragement and approval.

In the depression that followed the receipt of this letter he was no match for Roldan. He even himself took a caravel and sailed towards Xaragua, where he was met by Roldan, who boarded his ship and made his new proposals. Their impudence is astounding; and when we consider that the Admiral had in theory absolute powers in the island, the fact that such proposals could be made, not to say accepted, shows how far out of relation were his actual with his nominal powers. Roldan proposed that he should be allowed to give a number of his friends a free passage to Spain; that to all who should remain free grants of land should be given; and (a free pardon and certificate of good conduct contenting him no longer) that a proclamation should be made throughout the island admitting that all the charges of disloyalty and mutiny which had been brought against him and his followers were without foundation; and, finally, that he should be restored to his office of Alcalde Mayor or chief magistrate.

Here was a bolus for Christopher to swallow; a bolus compounded of his own words, his own acts, his hope, dignity, supremacy. In dismal humiliation he accepted the terms, with the addition of a clause more scandalous still—to the effect that the mutineers reserved the right, in case the Admiral should fail in the exact performance of any of his promises, to enforce them by compulsion of arms or any other method they might think fit. This precious document was signed on September 28, 1499 just twelve months after the agreement which it was intended to replace; and the Admiral, sailing dismally back to San Domingo, ruefully pondered on the fruits of a year's delay. Even then he was trying to make excuses for himself, such as he made afterwards to the Sovereigns when he tried to explain that this shameful capitulation was invalid. That he signed under compulsion; that he was on board a ship, and so was not on his viceregal territory; that the rebels had already been tried, and that he had not the power to revoke a sentence which bore the authority of the Crown; that he had not the power to dispose of the Crown property —desperate, agonised shuffling of pride and self-esteem in the coils of trial and difficulty. Enough of it.

CHAPTER VI

AN INTERLUDE

A breath of salt air again will do us no harm as a relief from these perilous balancings of Columbus on the see-saw at Espanola. His true work in this world had indeed already been accomplished. When he smote the rock of western discovery many springs flowed from it, and some were destined to run in mightier channels than that which he himself followed. Among other men stirred by the news of Columbus's first voyage there was one walking the streets of Bristol in 1496 who was fired to a similar enterprise—a man of Venice, in boyhood named Zuan Caboto, but now known in England, where he has some time been settled, as Captain John Cabot. A sailor and trader who has travelled much through the known sea-roads of this world, and has a desire to travel upon others not so well known. He has been in the East, has seen the caravans of Mecca and the goods they carried, and, like Columbus, has conceived in his mind the roundness of the world as a practical fact rather than a mere mathematical theory. Hearing of Columbus's success Cabot sets what machinery in England he has access to in motion to secure for him patents from King Henry VII.; which patents he receives on March 5, 1496. After spending a long time in preparation, and being perhaps a little delayed by diplomatic protests from the Spanish Ambassador in London, he sails from Bristol in May 1497.

After sailing west two thousand leagues Cabot found land in the neighbourhood of Cape Breton, and was thus in all probability the first discoverer, since the Icelanders, of the mainland of the New World. He turned northward, sailed through the strait of Belle Isle, and came home again, having accomplished his task in three months. Cabot, like Columbus, believed he had seen the territory of the Great Khan, of whom he told the interested population of Bristol some strange things. He further told them of the probable riches of this new land if it were followed in a southerly direction; told them some lies also, it appears, since he said that the waters there were so dense with fish that his vessels could hardly move in them. He received a gratuity of L10 and a pension, and made a great sensation in Bristol by walking about the city dressed in fine silk garments. He took other voyages also with his son Sebastian, who followed with him the rapid widening stream of discovery and became Pilot Major of Spain, and President of the Congress appointed in 1524 to settle the conflicting pretensions of various discoverers; but so far as our narrative is concerned, having sailed across from Bristol and discovered the mainland of the New World some years before Columbus discovered it, John Cabot sails into oblivion.

Another great conquest of the salt unknown taken place a few days before Columbus sailed on his third voyage. The accidental discovery of the Cape by Bartholomew Diaz in 1486 had not been neglected by Portugal; and the achievements of Columbus, while they cut off Portuguese enterprise from the western ocean, had only stimulated it to greater activity within its own spheres. Vasco da Gama sailed from Lisbon in July 1497; by the end of November he had rounded the Cape of Good Hope; and in May 1498, after a long voyage full of interest, peril, and hardship he had landed at Calicut on the shores of the true India. He came back in 1499 with a battered remnant, his crew disabled by sickness and exhaustion, and half his ships lost; but he had in fact discovered a road for trade and adventure to the East that was not paved with promises, dreams, or mad affidavits, but was a real and tangible achievement, bringing its reward in commerce and wealth for Portugal. At that very moment Columbus was groping round the mainland of South America, thinking it to be the coast of Cathay, and the Garden of Eden, and God knows what other cosmographical—theological abstractions; and Portugal, busy with her arrangements for making money, could afford for the moment to look on undismayed at the development of the mine of promises discovered by the Spanish Admiral.

The anxiety of Columbus to communicate the names of things before he had made sure of their substance received another rude chastisement in the events that followed the receipt in Spain of his letter announcing the discovery of the Garden of Eden and the land of pearls. People in Spain were not greatly interested in his theories of the terrestrial Paradise; but more than one adventurer pricked up his ears at the name of pearls, and among the first was our old friend Alonso de Ojeda, who had returned some time before from Espanola and was living in Spain. His position as a member of Columbus's force on the second voyage and the distinction he had gained there gave him special opportunities of access to the letters and papers sent home by Columbus; and he found no difficulty in getting Fonseca to show him the maps and charts of the coast of Paria sent back by the Admiral, the veritable pearls which had been gathered, and the enthusiastic descriptions of the wealth of this new coast. Knowing something of Espanola, and of the Admiral also, and reading in the despatches of the turbulent condition of the colony, he had a shrewd idea that Columbus's hands would be kept pretty full in Espanola itself, and that he would have no opportunity for some time to make any more voyages of discovery. He therefore represented to Fonseca what a pity it would be if all this revenue should remain untapped just because one man had not time to attend to it, and he proposed that he should take out an expedition at his own cost and share the profits with the Crown.

17

This proposal was too tempting to be refused; unlike the expeditions of Columbus, which were all expenditure and no revenue, it promised a chance of revenue without any expenditure at all. The Paria coast, having been discovered subsequent to the agreement made with Columbus, was considered by Fonseca to be open to private enterprise; and he therefore granted Ojeda a licence to go and explore it. Among those who went with him were Amerigo Vespucci and Columbus's old pilot, Juan de la Cosa, as well as some of the sailors who had been with the Admiral on the coast of Paria and had returned in the caravels which had brought his account of it back to Spain. Ojeda sailed on May 20, 1499; made a landfall some hundreds of miles to the eastward of the Orinoco, coasted thence as far as the island of Trinidad, and sailed along the northern coast of the peninsula of Paria until he came to a country where the natives built their hots on piles in the water, and to which he gave the name of Venezuela. It was by his accidental presence on this voyage that Vespucci, the meat-contractor, came to give his name to America—a curious story of international jealousies, intrigues, lawsuits, and lies which we have not the space to deal with here. After collecting a considerable quantity of pearls Ojeda, who was beginning to run short of provisions, turned eastward again and sought the coast of Espanola, where we shall presently meet with him again.

And Ojeda was not the only person in Spain who was enticed by Columbus's glowing descriptions to go and look for the pearls of Paria. There was in fact quite a reunion of old friends of his and ours in the western ocean, though they went thither in a spirit far different from that of ancient friendship. Pedro Alonso Nino, who had also been on the Paria coast with Columbus, who had come home with the returning ships, and whose patience (for he was an exceedingly practical man) had perhaps been tried by the strange doings of the Admiral in the Gulf of Paria, decided that he as well as any one else might go and find some pearls. Nino is a poor man, having worked hard in all his voyagings backwards and forwards across the Atlantic; but he has a friend with money, one Luis Guerra, who provides him with the funds necessary for fitting out a small caravel about the size of his old ship the Nifta. Guerra, who has the money, also has a brother Christoval; and his conditions are that Christoval shall be given the command of the caravel. Practical Niflo does not care so long as he reaches the place where the pearls are. He also applies to Fonseca for licence to make discoveries; and, duly receiving it, sails from Palos in the beginning of June 1499, hot upon the track of Ojeda.

They did a little quiet discovery, principally in the domain of human nature, caroused with the friendly natives, but attended to business all the time; with the result that in the following April they were back in Spain with a treasure of pearls out of which, after Nifio had been made independent for life and Guerra, Christoval, and the rest of them had their shares, there remained a handsome sum for the Crown. An extremely practical, businesslike voyage this; full of lessons for our poor Christopher, could he but have known and learned them.

Yet another of our old friends profited by the Admiral's discovery. What Vincenti Yafiez Pinzon has been doing all these years we have no record; living at Palos, perhaps, doing a little of his ordinary coasting business, administering the estates of his brother Martin Alonso, and, almost for a certainty, talking pretty big about who it was that really did all the work in the discovery of the New World. Out of the obscurity of conjecture he emerges into fact in December 1499, when he is found at Palos fitting out four caravels for the purpose of exploring farther along the coast of the southern mainland. That he also was after pearls is pretty certain; but on the other hand he was more of a sailor than an adventurer, was a discoverer at heart, and had no small share of the family taste for sea travel. He took a more southerly course than any of the others and struck the coast of America south of the equator on January 20, 1500. He sailed north past the mouths of the Amazon and Orinoco through the Gulf of Paria, and reached Espanola in June 1500. He only paused there to take in provisions, and sailed to the west in search of further discoveries; but he lost two of his caravels in a gale and had to put back to Espanola.

He sailed thence for Palos, and reached home in September 1500, having added no inconsiderable share to the mass of new geographical knowledge that was being accumulated. In later years he took a high place in the maritime world of Spain.

And finally, to complete the account of the chief minor discoveries of these two busy years, we must mention Pedro Alvarez Cabral of Portugal, who was despatched in March 1, 1500 from Lisbon to verify the discoveries of Da Gama. He reached Calicut six months later, losing on the voyage four of his caravels and most of his company. Among the lost was Bartholomew Diaz, the first discoverer of the Cape of Good Hope, who was on this voyage in a subordinate capacity, and whose bones were left to dissolve in the stormy waters that beat round the Cape whose barrier he was the first to pass. The chief event of this voyage, however, was not the reaching of Calicut nor the drowning of Diaz (which was chiefly of importance to himself, poor soul!) but the discovery of Brazil, which Cabral made in following the southerly course too far to the west. He landed there, in the Bay of Porto Seguro, on May 1, 1500, and took formal possession of the land for the Crown of Portugal, naming it Vera Cruz, or the Land of the True Cross.

In the assumption of Columbus and his contemporaries all these doings were held to detract from the glory of his own achievements, and were the subject of endless affidavits, depositions, quarrels, arguments, proofs and claims in the great lawsuit that was in after years carried on between the Crown of Spain and the heirs of Columbus concerning his titles and revenues. We, however, may take a different view. With the exception of the discoveries of the Cape of Good Hope and the coast of Brazil all these enterprises were directly traceable to Columbus's own achievements and were inspired by his example. The things that a man can do in his own person are limited by the laws of time and space; it is only example and influence that are infinite and illimitable, and in which the spirit of any achievement can find true immortality.

CHAPTER VII

THE THIRD VOYAGE-(continued)

It may perhaps be wearisome to the reader to return to the tangled and depressing situation in Espanola, but it cannot be half so wearisome as it was for Columbus, whom we left enveloped in that dark cloud of error and surrender in which he sacrificed his dignity and good faith to the impudent demands of a mutinous servant. To his other troubles in San Domingo the presence of this Roldan was now added; and the reinstated Alcalde was not long in making use of the victory he had gained. He bore himself with intolerable arrogance and insolence, discharging one of Columbus's personal bodyguard on the ground that no one should hold any office on the island except with his consent. He demanded grants of land for himself and his followers, which Columbus held himself obliged to concede; and the Admiral, further to pacify him, invented a very disastrous system of repartimientos, under which certain chiefs were relieved from paying tribute on condition of furnishing feudal service to the settlers—a system which rapidly developed into the most cruel and oppressive kind of slavery. The Admiral at this time also, in despair of keeping things quiet by his old methods of peace and conciliation, created a kind of police force which roamed about the island, exacting tribute and meting out summary punishment to all defaulters. Among other concessions weakly made to Roldan at this time was the gift of the Crown estate of Esperanza, situated in the Vega Real, whither he betook himself and embarked on what was nothing more nor less than a despotic reign, entirely ignoring the regulations and prerogatives of the Admiral, and taking prisoners and administering punishment just as he pleased. The Admiral was helpless, and thought of going back to Spain, but the condition of the island was such that he did not dare to leave it. Instead, he wrote a long letter to the Sovereigns, full of complaints against other people and justifications of himself, in the course of which he set forth those quibbling excuses for his capitulation to Roldan which we have already heard. And there was a pathetic request at the end of the letter that his son Diego might be sent out to him. As I have said, Columbus was by this time a prematurely old man, and feeling the clouds gathering about him, and the loneliness and friendlessness of his position at Espanola, he instinctively looked to the next generation for help, and to the presence of his own son for sympathy and comfort.

It was at this moment (September 5, 1499) that a diversion arose in the rumour that four caravels had been seen off the western end of Espanola and duly reported to the Admiral; and this announcement was soon followed by the news that they were commanded by Ojeda, who was collecting dye-wood in the island forests. Columbus, although he had so far as we know had no previous difficulties with Ojeda, had little cause now to credit any adventurer with kindness towards himself; and Ojeda's secrecy in not reporting himself at San Domingo, and, in fact, his presence on the island at all without the knowledge of the Admiral, were sufficient evidence that he was there to serve his own ends. Some gleam of Christopher's old cleverness in handling men was—now shown by his instructing Roldan to sally forth and bring Ojeda to order. It was a case of setting a thief to catch a thief and, as it turned out, was not a bad stroke. Roldan, nothing loth, sailed round to that part of the coast where Ojeda's ships were anchored, and asked to see his licence; which was duly shown to him and rather took the wind out of his sails. He heard a little gossip from Ojeda, moreover, which had its own significance for him. The Queen was ill; Columbus was in disgrace; there was talk of superseding him. Ojeda promised to sail round to San Domingo and report himself; but instead, he sailed to the east along the coast of Xaragua, where he got into communication with some discontented Spanish settlers and concocted a scheme for leading them to San Domingo to demand redress for their imagined grievances. Roldan, however, who had come to look for Ojeda, discovered him at this point; and there ensued some very pretty play between the two rascals, chiefly in trickery and treachery, such as capturing each other's boats and emissaries, laying traps for one another, and taking prisoner one another's crews. The end of it was that Ojeda left the island without having reported himself to Columbus, but not before he had completed his business—which was that of provisioning his ships and collecting dye-wood and slaves.

And so exit Ojeda from the Columbian drama. Of his own drama only one more act remained to be played; which, for the sake of our past interest in him, we will mention here. Chiefly on account of his intimacy with Fonseca he was some years later given a governorship in the neighbourhood of the Gulf of Darien; Juan de la Cosa accompanying him as unofficial partner. Ojeda has no sooner landed there than he is fighting the natives; natives too many for him this time; Ojeda forced to hide in the forest, where he finds the body of de la Cosa, who has come by a shocking death. Ojeda afterwards tries to govern his colony, but is no good at that; cannot govern his own temper, poor fellow. Quarrels with his crew, is put in irons, carried to Espanola, and dies there (1515) in great poverty and eclipse. One of the many, evidently, who need a strong guiding hand, and perish without it.

It really began to seem as though Roldan, having had his fling and secured the excessive privileges that he coveted, had decided that loyalty to Christopher was for the present the most profitable policy; but the mutinous spirit that he had cultivated in his followers for his own ends could not be so readily converted into this cheap loyalty. More trouble was yet to come of this rebellion. There was in the island a young Spanish aristocrat, Fernando de Guevara by name, one of the many who had come out in the hope of enjoying himself and making a fortune quickly, whose more than outrageously dissolute life in San Domingo had caused Columbus to banish him thence; and he was now living near Xaragua with a cousin of his, Adrian de Moxeca, who had been one of the ringleaders in Roldan's conspiracy. Within this pleasant province of Xaragua lived, as we have seen, Anacaona, the sister of Caonabo, the Lord of the House of Gold. She herself was a beautiful woman, called by her subjects Bloom of the Gold; and she had a still more beautiful daughter, Higuamota, who appears in history, like so many other women, on account of her charms and what came of them.

Of pretty Higuamota, who once lived like a dryad among the groves of Espanola and has been dead now for so long, we know nothing except that she was beautiful, which, although she doubtless did not think so while she lived, turns out to have been the most important thing about her. Young Guevara, coming to stay with his cousin Adrian, becomes a visitor at the house of Anacaona; sees the pretty daughter and falls in love with her. Other people also, it appears, have been in a similar state, but Higuamota is not very accessible; a fact which of course adds to the interest of the chase, and turns dissolute Fernando's idle preference into something like a passion. Roldan, who has also had an eye upon her, and apparently no more than an eye, discovers that Fernando, in order to gratify his passion, is proposing to go the absurd length of marrying the young woman, and has sent for a priest for that purpose. Roldan, instigated thereto by primitive forces, thinks it would be impolitic for a Spanish grandee to marry with a heathen; very well, then, Fernando will have her baptized—nothing simpler when water and a priest are handy. Roldan, seeing that the young man is serious, becomes peremptory, and orders him to leave Xaragua. Fernando ostentatiously departs, but is discovered a little later actually living in the house of Anacaona, who apparently is sympathetic to Love's young dream. Once more ordered away, this time with anger and threats, Guevara changes his tune and implores Roldan to let him stay, promising that he will give up the marriage project and also, no doubt, the no-marriage project. But Guevara has sympathisers. The mutineers have not forgiven Roldan for deserting them and becoming a lawful instead of an unlawful ruler. They are all on the side of Guevara, who accordingly moves to the next stage of island procedure, and sets on foot some kind of plot to kill Roldan and the Admiral. Fortunately where there is treachery it generally works both ways; this plot came to the ears of the authorities; the conspirators were arrested and sent to San Domingo.

This action came near to bringing the whole island about Columbus's ears. Adrian de Moxeca was furious at what he conceived to be the treachery of Roldan, for Roldan was in such a pass that the barest act of duty was necessarily one of treachery to his friends. Moxeca took the place of chief rebel that Roldan had vacated; rallied the mutineers round him, and was on the point of starting for Concepcion, one of the chain of forts across the island where Columbus was at present staying, when the Admiral discovered his plan. All that was strongest and bravest in him rose up at this menace. His weakness and cowardice were forgotten; and with the spirit of an old sea-lion he sallied forth against the mutineers. He had only a dozen men on whom he could rely, but he armed them well and marched secretly and swiftly under cloud of night to the place where Moxeca and his followers were encamped in fond security, and there suddenly fell upon them, capturing Moxeca and the chief ringleaders. The rest scattered in terror and escaped. Moxeca was hurried off to the battlements of San Domingo and there, in the very midst of a longdrawn trembling confession to the priest in attendance, was swung off the ramparts and hanged. The others, although also condemned to death, were kept in irons in the fortress, while Christopher and Bartholomew, roused at last to vigorous action, scoured the island hunting down the remainder, killing some who resisted, hanging others on the spot, and imprisoning the remainder at San Domingo.

After these prompt measures peace reigned for a time in the island, and Columbus was perhaps surprised to see what wholesome effects could be produced by a little exemplary severity. The natives, who under the weakness of his former rule had been discontented and troublesome, now settled down submissively to their yoke; the Spaniards began to work in earnest on their farms; and there descended upon island affairs a brief St. Martin's Summer of peace before the final winter of blight and death set in. The Admiral, however, was obviously in precarious health; his ophthalmia became worse, and the stability of his mind suffered. He had dreams and visions of divine help and comfort, much needed by him, poor soul, in all his tribulations and adversities. Even yet the cup was not full.

We must now turn back to Spain and try to form some idea of the way in which the doings of Columbus were being regarded there if we are to understand the extraordinary calamity that was soon to befall him. It must be remembered first of all that his enterprise had never really been popular from the first. It was carried out entirely by the energy and confidence of Queen Isabella, who almost alone of those in power believed in it as a thing which was certain to bring ultimate glory, as well as riches and dominion, to Spain and the Catholic faith. As we have seen, there had been a brief ebullition of popular favour when Columbus returned from his first voyage, but it was a popularity excited solely by the promises of great wealth that Columbus was continually holding forth. When those promises were not immediately fulfilled popular favour subsided; and when the adventurers who had gone out to the new islands on the strength of those promises had returned with shattered health and empty pockets there was less chance than ever of the matter being regarded in its proper light by the people of Spain. Columbus had either found a gold mine or he had found nothing—that was the way in which the matter was popularly regarded. Those who really understood the significance of his discoveries and appreciated their scientific importance did not merely stay at home in Spain and raise a clamour; they went out in the Admiral's footsteps and continued the work that he had begun. Even King Ferdinand, for all his cleverness, had never understood the real lines on which the colony should have been developed. His eyes were fixed upon Europe; he saw in the discoveries of Columbus a means rather than an end; and looked to them simply as a source of revenue with the help of which he could carry on his ambitious schemes. And when, as other captains made voyages confirming and extending the work of Columbus, he did begin to understand the significance of what had been done, he realised too late that the Admiral had been given powers far in excess of what was prudent or sensible.

During all the time that Columbus and his brothers were struggling with the impossible situation at Espanola there was but one influence at work in Spain, and that was entirely destructive to the Admiral. Every caravel that came from the New World brought two things. It brought a crowd of discontented colonists, many of whom had grave reasons for their discontent; and it brought letters from the Admiral in which more and more promises were held out, but in which also querulous complaints against this and that person, and against the Spanish settlers generally, were set forth at wearisome length. It is not remarkable that the people of Spain, even those who were well disposed towards Columbus, began to wonder if these two things were not cause and effect. The settlers may have been a poor lot, but they were the material with which Columbus had to deal; he had powers enough, Heaven knew, powers of life and death; and the problem began to resolve itself in the minds of those at the head of affairs in Spain in the following terms. Given an island, rich and luxuriant beyond the dreams of man; given a native population easily subdued; given settlers of one kind or another; and given a Viceroy with unlimited powers—could he or could he not govern the island? It was a by no means unfair way of putting the case, and there is little justice in the wild abuse that has been hurled at Ferdinand and Isabella on this ground. Columbus may have been the greatest genius in the world; very possibly they admitted it; but in the meanwhile Spain was resounding with the cries of the impoverished colonists who had returned from his ocean Paradise. No doubt the Sovereigns ignored them as much as they possibly could; but when it came to ragged emaciated beggars coming in batches of fifty at a time and sitting in the very courts of the Alhambra, exhibiting bunches of grapes and saying that that was all they could afford to live upon since they had come back from the New World, some notice had to be taken of it. Even young Diego and Ferdinand, the Admiral's sons, came in for the obloquy with which his name was associated; the colonial vagabonds hung round the portals of the palace and cried out upon them as they passed so that they began to dislike going out. Columbus, as we know, had plenty of enemies who had access to the King and Queen; and never had enemies an easier case to urge. Money was continually being spent on ships and supplies; where was the return for it? What about the Ophir of Solomon? What about the Land of Spices? What about the pearls? And if you want to add a touch of absurdity, what about the Garden of Eden and the Great Khan?

To the most impartial eyes it began to appear as though Columbus were either an impostor or a fool. There is no evidence that Ferdinand and Isabella thought that he was an impostor or that he had wilfully deceived them; but there is some evidence that they began to have an inkling as to what kind of a man he really was, and as to his unfitness for governing a colony. Once more something had to be done. The sending out of a commissioner had not been a great success before, but in the difficulties of the situation it seemed the only thing. Still there was a good deal of hesitation, and it is probable that Isabella was not yet fully convinced of the necessity for this grave step. This hesitation was brought to an end by the arrival from Espanola of the ships bearing the followers of Roldan, who had been sent back under the terms of Columbus's feeble capitulation. The same ships brought a great quantity of slaves, which the colonists were able to show had been brought by the permission of the Admiral; they carried native girls also, many of them pregnant, many with new-born babies; and these also came with the permission of the Admiral. The ships further carried the Admiral's letter complaining of the conspiracy of Roldan and containing the unfortunate request for a further licence to extend the slave trade. These circumstances were probably enough to turn the scale of Isabella's opinion against the Admiral's administration. The presence of the slaves particularly angered her kind womanly heart. "What right has he to give away my vassals?" she exclaimed, and ordered that they should all be sent back, and that in addition all the other slaves who had come home should be traced and sent back; although of course it was impossible to carry out this last order.

At any rate there was no longer any hesitation about sending out a commissioner, and the Sovereigns chose one Francisco de Bobadilla, an official of the royal household, for the performance of this difficult mission. As far as we can decipher him he was a very ordinary official personage; prejudiced, it is possible, against an administration that had produced such disastrous results and which offended his orderly official susceptibilities; otherwise to be regarded as a man exactly honest in the performance of what he conceived to be his duties, and entirely indisposed to allow sentiment or any other extraneous matter to interfere with such due performance. We shall have need to remember, when we see him at work in Espanola, that he was not sent out to judge between Columbus and his Sovereigns or between Columbus and the world, but to investigate the condition of the colony and to take what action he thought necessary. The commission which he bore to the Admiral was in the following terms:

"The King and the Queen: Don Christopher Columbus, our Admiral of the Ocean-sea. We have directed Francisco de Bobadilla, the bearer of this, to speak to you for us of certain things which he will mention: we request you to give him faith and credence and to obey him. From Madrid, May 26, '99. I THE KING. I THE QUEEN. By their command. Miguel Perez de Almazan."

In addition Bobadilla bore with him papers and authorities giving him complete control and possession of all the forts, arms, and royal property in the island, in case it should be necessary for him to use them; and he also had a number of blank warrants which were signed, but the substance of which was not filled in. This may seem very dreadful to us, with our friendship for the poor Admiral; but considering the grave state of affairs as represented to the King and Queen, who had their duties to their colonial subjects as well as to Columbus, there was nothing excessive in it. If they were to send out a commissioner at all, and if they were satisfied, as presumably they were, that the man they had chosen was trustworthy, it was only right to make his authority absolute. Thus equipped Francisco de Bobadilla sailed from Spain in July 1500.

The End